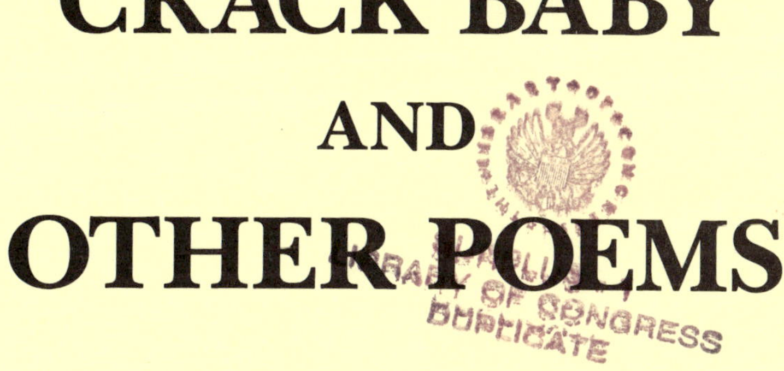

CRACK BABY AND OTHER POEMS

Crack Baby

and

Other Poems

Addie Lee

White Dogwood Press

Library of Congress Catalog Card
Number: 89-90581
 Printed in the
United States of America. For information
write White Dogwood Press, P.O. Box 135,
Abington, PA 19001.
ISBN 0-9625139-0-3.

Illustrations by Elizabeth Duffy,
Beaver College, Glenside, PA 19038.

Printing by Wickersham Printing
Company, Inc., 2959 Old Tree Drive,
Lancaster, PA 17603-4080.

CONTENTS

ACKNOWLEDGMENTS

Acknowledgment is made to the following publications in which some of the selections appeared:

VOICES, Vinalhaven, Maine.

SOLSTICE, Philadelphia, Pennsylvania.

BROADWAY MUSIC PRODUCTIONS, Sarasota, Florida.

WELCOMAT, Philadelphia, Pennsylvania.

COOL TRAVELER, Philadelphia, Pennsylvania.

TALENT EXPO, Philadelphia, Pennsylvania.

THE PLOWMAN, INTERNATIONAL POETRY AND ART, and THE PLOWMAN ANTHOLOGY, Whitby, Ontario, Canada. Distributed in Australia, England, Canada, and the USA.

TEXTURES, Philadelphia, Pennsylvania.

CRACK BABY

Infant fingers curled too tight
screams and wails through the night
legs drawn stiffly to her chest
pain she cannot put to rest.

Hold her, rock her; now her brain
fills with tiny hemorrhages again.
At 2 A. M. she sleeps in bed—
Crack Baby lies blue and dead.

A SUMMER EVENING

Cicadas sing and pole lights gleam
as we rock on the floor of our wide front porch.
Couples walk in the soft languor
of evening air, while a neighbor's porch light
shines starlike through the green leaves of trees.

Years ago, we gathered at the corner,
told ghost stories and caught fireflies
to make rings for our fingers,
wove pink clover chains until the mosquitoes
and grass chiggers drove us in toward the call home.

Now at the corner, on mornings after,
empty crack vials strew the pavement.
Drug pushers and gang fights sprinkle the dark
with bullet whines and knife screams.
Children 'deal' because no one's at home.

We go inside, turn on the TV,
hear a barrage of killing and crime
on the late evening news, pad off to bed,
play the FM, Beethoven's *Pastorale*,
and wonder if we will be stabbed in our sleep.

ATHLETE

Like some modern discus thrower,
that golden haired boy
glinting in the sunlight
streaming down
through blown autumn leaves.
Myron caught the perfect moment,
that poised, balanced, graceful pose.
This youth possesses that same cool look,
his eyes full of promise,
intently fixed on the near goal.
His leg muscles quiver, then tauten;
he plants his feet
firmly on the ground,
aligns his center of gravity
with unconscious, precise flow.
His every move signals purpose,
strategic maneuvering
in an unseen game of chess.
Myron's Greek sculpture
captured a clean beautiful harmony,
mind and body swinging together
in pure unison and glorious anthem.
Olympic flames burn eternally
in this young athlete's turn and gaze
to a distant, faraway field
in some private, unknown land.

A ROSE LEAVED TEACUP

A tall, thin, aristocratic lady,
she sits swathed in shawls and lap rug,
her white wicker rocker
moving faintly against the tired boards
of her columned front porch.
Georgia fashions her lingering days
reading French novels
beneath a magnifying glass,
picking up garden sticks
to tie in small bundles,
and walking to town
clad in white gloves,
beribboned straw hat.

She lives alone in the family home,
her once rich father having failed
in business, a broken man long gone.
Her mother tried to clear his name,
to no avail, legal complexities.
Georgia wore out two typewriters
and became a recluse.
Her mother wore a sun hat,
painted Pennsylvania flowers
and open countrysides
in whites, pinks, blues, greens,
yellows and browns.
Wanting neither altar nor convent,
Georgia chose to stay on alone.
At night she leaves a light burning
in the triple hall windows
on the second floor
and wears a police whistle
around her neck.

Eighty-eight, her eyesight diminished,
she recalls the past tenaciously.
Days when her eyes are bad
and things disappear,
the gremlins, she whimsically says.
She tells endless stories
of the town's proud Quaker past,
the heyday of trolleys
and the Curtis Publishing Company,
Strawbridge and Clothier,
Wanamaker's Gallery,
her father's chess games,
the Old York Road Golf Club,
maple shaded Wyncote,
gray slate roofs and fieldstone walls,
the maid and housekeeper,
tonics for neurasthenia,
afternoon teas with polished silver,
bygone hours of violet, lace, and cream.

Then, the day when she fell on the stairs.
Her small dog Jacko
jumped through the window.
Georgia was taken to a convalescent home.
The house was sold
to pay her expenses,
her piano, furniture, china, and linens
auctioned to the highest bidder.
That was the way things had to be.
The obituary gave only
slender facts,
nothing of the whitebright memories,
the triple hall windows,
the rose leaved teacup,
the oil painting of white peonies
left behind to burnish me.

WYNCOTE ROAD

Moss covered stones
hugging the road curves,
flat, gray, irregular stones,
stone upon stone,
stone steps climbing the hill,
stepping stones
cutting across the grass,
stonewalled houses,
ivy covered stones,
resting stones.

Rhododendron, tall giants,
secluding old
storied houses
set far back,
away from the street.
White, pink, and rose-purple
flowers rioting profusely
through dark green heath.

Azalea, laurel, and yew
forming tall hedges
of berried evergreen
and blossoming bush.
Gardens running rife and wild,
an overgrown look,
yet cozying naturally
toward sky-reaching trees.

A settled air,
friends and neighbors
who coffee klatch and sing,
young and old,
some inbetween.
Road we have walked,
biked, and driven.
Children who played,
married, and scattered,
still to return
to roots deeper than any other,
bonds holding fast,
yet not forever.

RED GLORY

Flaming trees, October leaves
burning bushes warmed by the sun
pattern young minds
with golden red glory
and season's downfall.
So fast, the dry leaves
bare still alive branches
naked to winter winds and snowbirds;
so soon, compost to feed
the life-hungry earth.

The earth will be here
long after we are gone,
generations of leaves
and live green seedlings
trailing our passing.
Before going, we want to tell
those coming after to flower
the earth and leave behind
some memories of kindness,
testimony of care and peace.

Missouri Farm

a prose poem

MISSOURI FARM

Driving along a black asphalt road through the tiny village of Roanoke in Randolph County, Missouri, one comes to a country store with gasoline pumps out front, the Roanoke Community Church, the Roanoke Cemetery, an old-fashioned band stand (formerly the site of ice cream suppers and band concerts), a very small house which serves as combination post office and telephone office, and three or four stately two-story houses, the kind with lace curtains at the windows, rockers on the front porch, colorful long flower boxes, and red and purple petunia pots. It's best to drive slowly as a dog may cross the road, seemingly unaware of Toyotas and the passing of time.

A half mile out of town, sitting beyond the left fork in the road, the old country schoolhouse still stands. No longer in use, it nestles patiently like a tired horse, freed from the harness and allowed to stand in the shade of an old cottonwood tree. The weeds around the schoolhouse yard have been cut down by someone with a hand sickle, and the cock high up on the weathervaned steeple of the schoolhouse proudly struts and peaks in the changing winds.

Two miles out of Roanoke, my grandfather's farm springs into view. Over the hills, set against the sky, I first glimpse the steep downward sloping roof of the red barn, the white house with its long low spread, cluster of small sheds, the cattle pond in the front pasture, and the whitewashed rail fence surrounding the farmhouse flanked in by cedar, sycamore, oak, and mulberry trees.

As I approach the gravel drive and swing open the limber white gate, I pause, wondering if this can still be my grandfather's farm. As in a dream, I move my hands over the sun-blistered boards. Gone are the careless hours when I walked that fence, barefoot and confident, joyful, strong, spirited, and free. How keenly I remember. To the left of the fence, a Red River—to the right, a Black Valley. To step on a crack would break my mother's back. I lived happily then. Now the sun shines brightly, a glorious red crescendo dazzling my eyes. It shifts and changes, yellow, orange, red, blinding my sight when I steal a glance.

I walk to the front porch of the farmhouse and sit on the hard benches, then move to the rocker. On the old elm tree I detect a piece of gray frayed rope tied in a knot to one of the high upper branches, only the knot remaining of a long thick rope from which hung a smooth tire swing. My cousin once told me that a lone Confederate soldier had hung himself from that same branch, but I never believed it. Jamie was like that, always telling stories. We used to argue about whose turn it was to draw water from the well. Even now I see the water suddenly gushing forth as I turn the battered handle and listen to the creaking chains. I have no bucket or tin dipper. It doesn't matter. The well has gone dry. No dogs come running or lie yawning in the sun. No yellow, black, white, or spotted kittens play around the rocky corners of the empty dilapidated farmhouse.

I take the brick path to the wash house and smokehouse. Slowly I begin to see my grandmother standing over huge iron vats and kettles, the wash water boiling hot. Wooden sticks and lye soap churn up the steam. My father, a little boy, falls against the hot cauldron, his back and chest ringed by the steam and scalding bubbles, the skin consumed. My grandmother stays up through the night beating egg whites to pour over the baked wet flesh. Years later, I saw cooked skin like that, after Hiroshima. Nausea overpowers me, and I lean against the garden gate.

The smokehouse no longer smells of smoke. I remember the days when whole hams hung from the rafters. Crocks of all sizes sat on the cool floor. They brimmed full of sausages, cracklings, pickled pigs' feet, head cheese, blood pudding. I liked the sausage and gagged at the rest.

I go through another gate to the henhouse, brooderhouse, ice house, red barn, and harness shed. Child that I once was, I sometimes went with my grandmother to gather the eggs. I never understood how she could reach under a hen and take the eggs without disturbing the old cluck, but my grandmother did. I seldom climbed down the ladder in the ice house with her to gather the eggs on the straw beneath. The hens sometimes laid eggs there. Blacksnakes lay hidden.

I walk away from the ice house and pass through still a third gate. Always on a farm there are so many gates to open and close. The sun gradually mounts in the sky as I enter the harness shed, still as mysterious as it once seemed with its singular skylight and warm dirt floor. I run my hands over the dented worktable, many pieces of harness, and leather reins smelling of sweat, grease, and the earth. Like a blind person, I want to feel everything left in the shed with the tips of my fingers. I press my damp face into the smoothness of an old leather saddle and clench my hand in the rough woolen cloth of a horse blanket. In my memory I hear Whitefoot nicker and Big Clyde answer. Sheep bleat and crowd the fence, cowbells clank, and hoof-prints in the mud slowly fill with water. Sunlight streams in through an open door of the harness shed and breaks my reverie.

I turn to the open fields and orchards. Cherry ripe, the song still sings, tingling my ear. Peaches swell to scarlet gold. Plums hang in juicy balls of purple, blue, and red. Yellow apples grow round and mellow. I want the freshness, the flavor, the color, the richness, and the glory of the farm to return. The sun reaches its zenith.

Out in the fields the sun shines mercilessly. The rich black bottomland soil absorbs the heat and yields heaping crops. I look up the lane where wagonloads of wheat toiled down. My eyes blur as the iron wheels jog in the ruts, teams of horses pulling hard at their traces. The blinders, collars, reins, and bridles darken with effort. The leather dampens.

My grandfather shouts to Frank and Fanny and makes sucking noises with his tongue between his teeth. It's harvest time, and the threshers work until nine in the evening. Threshing machines drone and puff like belching monsters. Whites and blacks work side by side in the grimy dust. Red bandannas hang from their pockets, blue bib overalls darken with sweat, and stout leather shoes with knotted laces drag through the earth. I see the tired faces of the straw hat threshers trenched in dirt, outlined against the reddening sky, yellow fields bursting, the sun ablaze. Land of sorrow and land of joy, strawstacks like giants in a sky of glory.

The sun sinks slowly. My grandfather, Reuben, and Leon ride in the wagon that comes down the lane. Hired hands, neighbors, and friends shout greetings. Farm by farm, the threshers work in close community fashion. I hear the laughter of happy children. Tib, Jubie, and Jinsey scurry past carrying water jugs and canvased canteens. They smile with ivory teeth at Jamie and me. We join their wild games. My grandmother appears at the door of the farmhouse, my aunts, uncles, and cousins gathered around her. The sun is setting. The sky has reddened.

I walk at last to the top of a hill behind the barn. I find a familiar grassy mound, the same small gray stone marking the resting place of my grandmother's firstborn. I too bear that name. Missouri farm. Skies redden as they die. The day ends. Night comes. Young and strong, the spirit of the farm lives on.

GIVING THINGS

We fling our bodies
into piles of crackling leaves,
tumble and roll
in high drifts of fresh snow,
dive into ocean waves
that spring in giant leaps,
  knowing these things
  will break our collide.

Roots and stalks
push through the damp earth,
fruits and flowers
fill harvest baskets full,
sun and rain
feed the dark, hungry ground,
  all things ripen
  before they drop down.

Giving or receiving,
the path looks straight and clear,
through an open doorway
voices ring and call,
hearts slide into oneness
hands open and draw,
  when the earth yields beneath us,
  the price of giving is fall.

LORD OF THE PARK

Every day the two of them come,
the boy in the cap
and a lonely old gentleman.
The boy climbs a giant white oak;
the man heads for a wooden park bench.

Across the way, the railway station master
looks at his pocket watch
and trundles mailbags across a platform.
Passengers huddle, clasp their arms,
stare with blank eyes
for long awaited arrivals and departures.

Behind the depot on sunwarmed days
the wind riffles golden leaves
into tiny sailboats that glide
through the air in feathery rides.
The boy climbs high to his treeclouds.
There he reigns, lord of the park.

All aboard, the train conductor booms.
The boy's ears tingle.
He dreams of horses and dashing riders
swinging long booted legs into the stirrups.
The train gathers speed,
a flying steed of fast moving energy and light.

The boy's grandfather dozes on the park bench,
a walking stick across his knees,
his dream nodding toward yesterday's kingdoms,
his own lost boyhood and autumn love.
The curving long line of the train
recedes in the daylight,
distant, like a remembered embrace.

November crispness fills the air.
The silvery steel train tracks
shine in the sun's late afternoon light.
Hand in hand, the boy and the man
climb the station's darkening hill.
Together they begin the long walk home.

THE TREEHOUSE

Cleaning my window, I hear his weeping.
The young boy next door climbs to his treehouse,
and there in a hush of sunblotched leaves
his words fall in bright drops upon my face.
"They don't understand . . .
he's going away, far away."

A wren sings carols from the telephone pole.
The rag in my hand shows smudges of dirt.
Yesterday's paper notes the departure
of Mr. Charles Shelling for a position
teaching music in a Connecticut college.

His parents have told him that people
come and go. . . . Mostly go.
His friends have penknifed the case of his violin
rancorously and savagely with a jagged C. S.
Tree leaves sway in the soft, lilting breeze.

I listen silently from my window post,
shrouded behind the thin gauze of a curtain.
Clouds cover the sun; the wren still carols.
I do not feel now like glasswaxing the window.
I cannot see it through a hot welling swash.

MARIA

My mom has blown this lonesome town;
she says she's tired of feeling down.
Her skin was soft and olive brown.

Carlo and I have a secret plan.
We're going to find her and 'the man'
who gave her gold and a silken fan.

'The man' dealt on Second Street,
then vanished, a ghost on silent feet
when police arrived to walk the beat.

How she could leave us, we don't know—
cocaine could stop her from swinging low.
When the man came, she wanted to go.

We pray to the Virgin up in the sky
to shelter our mother and not let her die.
Carlo goes hungry; time passes by.

FIRST SNOW

Cold white winter moon,
shining through the windowpane,
transfixes this starscattered night.
Snow showers coat the earth,
turn the lamp posts
to thin white ghosts,
the hemlock branches
to lowslung fringed curtains.
We stand bewitched
in this pure, glistening kingdom,
this soundless, deep white fairyland.

Even as we watch, the flurried storm
buries our hedge in robes of whiteness.
A small hand slips into mine.
I promise him sledding and tell how,
when I was a boy, we cut our own
Christmas trees in the dark woods
behind the farm,
skated on the moonlit frozen pond
until our cherryred, stinging cheeks
drove us from the night's black ice.

Tomorrow morning I will have to dig
my way to the garden gate
in kneehigh boots, brush off the mailbox,
shovel the walks, and search
like a hound for the morning paper.
But now, this moment is ours,
first snow of a holy festive season.
His spellbound delight unfetters
memories and forgotten dreams.
Snowdrops will melt on my hair as I
clear the path for the morning milkman.

THE DISPOSSESSED

Justice wears a blindfold.
In singular bursts and energy streams
a challenger speaks
for the powerless and dispossessed.

Outstripping the bright light
of a noonday sun,
she pleads her cause
with masterful flings,
defender and intercessor
for homeless men with frozen feet,
bag ladies talking to voices from the past,
children molested, beaten, and abused.

Listening, I tighten my breath,
caught by the principle and passion
limned in her pleas.
Luminous dark eyes
press forward against the bar.
Words strike home,
perfectly bowed.
Riveted by charisma and grace,
I bite my lip on the difference to me.

When I chance to see her pray,
her hands folded
like soft flower petals on thin stalks,
knees bent in silken sheen,
her silent prayer tautens my throat,
tilts my careful neutrality.

Silent, hung up in chaliced skeins,
I find a paraclete
who feeds me a dream,
who makes life different
with aim well spent,
whose bold spiritual gaze
pierces the dark sun.

ORDINARY MATTERS

You ask why
I like to walk the dog,
cook the lasagna,
rake dry leaves,
and fold the laundry.
I reply,
common things
give me time,
moments of time,
to think about
some sky blue
morning-glory truth,
the apostolic sepals
of a passionflower vine
melding me
into perfect concrescence.

THE UNICORN

A unicorn stands on his smooth oak dresser,
glazed china figurine like the whiteness of Paul.
"Gift for me," he shyly said, "from a magic land,"
when he nudged it neighing against his cheek,
mythical visitor of childhood dreams.

With knights of old, medieval scenes
this youth unveiled his cast of mind.
I wander now in vacant rooms,
my young man gone in an armored tide,
his flag-draped cross battle sworn.

They sent ribbons and a Medal of Honor
which lie quietly inside the drawer
beside his neatly pressed uniform.
What land does the mort of his bugle keep?
Born to an early death, so fast the rose.

A low sun gleams on the unicorn's horn;
distant drums break a fading dream.
The hollows in my ears burn
as I fold his bodiless coat on the chair.
His last letter spoke about coming home.

BEULAH

Beulah's brown hands stir the warm oatmeal.
Her grandmother's breasts rise and fall.
She hums snatches of a hymn about the Promised Land;
her low croon brings Joey, Jake, and Nan,
Deserted crack babies from City Hospital.

In the New Age, the 1980's of Civilization,
Beulah lost her own three sons,
war in South Africa, A.I.D.S.,
and a New York City subway stabbing.

Life is hard in certain places.
She cannot turn the country around.
She doesn't have time to write her Congressmen.
Anger washes clean.

Beulah, mother to three, beats
the heartache plundering her soul.
Her eyes flow in rivers unseen
while Joey, Jake, and Nan
spoon, clap, smile, and sing.

PHILLY KILLING

If William Penn and Dr. King
could speak from their graves
about Robbie Williams and David Smith,
what would they say to the
City of Brotherly Love, where murder
has climbed higher than Franklin's kite?

Could their words stop the glut,
the market for cocaine,
or wildings and wolfpacks
from cruising the Green Town?
Would more police,
job training for dropouts,
woodlands and parks
convert the ashes of their dreams
to new Jerusalems and shining Camelots?

Drugs, knives, and hate destroy,
turn the arcades of Chestnut Street
into breeding grounds of roving teens,
their anger misspent in rawness of blood.
Where are the leaders,
the words of right stuff,
strategies that win,
dreams that don't die?

Bolting the door
won't turn things around.
There's no fast exit.
It's funneled down to you and me.

THE SOLDIER

You never know when it could hit.
No one is safe.
She brought him up with a sense of honor,
yet now she sits, numb at his bedside,
powerless to help or comfort.
She reads from his favorite book.
His eyes glaze, follow the rain
trickling down the closed window.
He falls asleep.

Transfused blood, perhaps,
when Army surgeons removed the bullet.
She tells herself it couldn't happen otherwise—
risky sex or shared drug needles,
not her son.
Her sister says
that war does things to people.

His friends drop in to say hello.
Now and then he moves his head,
inclines his face, listens faintly.
Droplets of sweat appear.
His temperature rises; his cough grows worse.
He doesn't know how it happened.
Doctors, nurses stand nearby.
Quietly, he breathes his last,
drops his arm in halfway salute.

STEPHEN FREIND

Christy wishes him screaming pain
childbirth twenty times twenty again,
thousands of diapers to Fab and clean
incest with an uncle, untold, unseen,
involuntary street rape, terror inhumane
manacles of poverty, misery insane.

Christy wonders if Mr. Freind has any plans
for battered children, trashed like tin cans.
Would he know what it is to be jerked around
or hung from rafters high above the ground?
Does he have any new child support scheme
or doesn't that count, a beggar's dream.

Christy sees a wide black crack;
hypocrisy deserves its own hard smack.
She sees a hole dark and deep,
Freind hitting bottom without a peep;
nor would Christy ever weep or mourn
for those who wish they had never been born.

INFINITY

William Blake wrote,
Our gods are our motives writ large.

For those who are wanted,
God first comes as a warm nuzzle,
a soft breast secreting colostrum,
a pair of hands unfolding,
reaching to hold us closer
than any receiving embrace again.
Then God comes as a paternal pat,
a proud look, a familiar back.

God sometimes comes
as a dazzling rainbow,
an arc of refracted sunrays
singing down the horizon's mist,
a weeping beech tree
hanging low to brush moist soil,
spreading water downward
to flower bushes of pearl.

Analysts say God is an illusion,
a wishful longing, a Linus blanket.
Theologians intone,
In the Beginning was the Word
and the Word was God.
Aren't we going in circles?
What's God? What's the Word?
What was the Beginning?

For some God wears a stallion's mane,
a shepherd's staff
crooked beneath his strong arm,
a staff hurled into a thunderbolt
or shaped to the bleating
heartbeat of a dove.

Some think God appears
on the island of Skorpios
in the gold plated bath
of a private yacht,
in the Trump Tower scraping
Manhattan's night sky
and bedded down
in filched Indian rock.

Books, legends say God even died
and came back to life in Osiris,
Jesus of Nazareth,
and the Manifestations of Brahma.
In every century,
God turns around,
wears a mask painted in colors,
black, white, yellow, and brown.

Some see God dressed in leather or satin,
stomping through Purple Rain,
swirling in psychedelic panoramas,
reeling through celluloid epic dramas,
God in micrographic imaging
unveiling medical mysteries
on a computer screen.

For those in pain,
God pops from a bottle
in a small white capsule.
All pain, every kind of pain,
stifled or stilled for a pause.
Alcohol helps swill it down
or a drop or two of water
from a radoned well.

Our small span of years
scarce makes one dot
in the eons of time.
Time, an invention or opportunity?
The universe, a creation or explosion?
Georgia O'Keeffe answers,
speaks in her bleached bone
ox skulls, red and brown hills,
showy white calla lilies.
In her austerity lives a dark peace.

SPACE

The age expands
astronauts moonwalk,
Sputnik seems light years ago.
Human frames
of watered dust
slip into orbit,
leave behind
earthbound views
for liftoff flights.
Past astronomies explode
and push beyond
to pitchy blue
and cold silence.
Twentieth century, the new physics,
someone says.
Shelter for the homeless,
food for starving Ethiopians,
cancer research, the ozone layer.
Space exploration
must go on, will go on.
Have to keep up with the Russians,
you know.
The planet or the universe,
our end is dark.
Cells will die,
but space goes on, the cosmos forever.
We count, blast off,
    search for unknown,
        distant supernovas.

THE SINGING DARK

Since we lay down, together slept,
quiet days have comforted me.

Your slender frame beneath the sheet
with strength of limb and lyric dream
has swelled my summer body proud.

Our growing child within me sings
this endless night I pass alone.

SONG

Red geraniums on my window sill
catch the morning light,
that quiet time of brightness
breaking through tall trees.

Mums massed along the wall
sway like ladies-in-waiting,
moving in long skirts of
lavender, yellow, and white.

Hanging bunches of scarlet berries
with tiny black bird eyes
weigh down the outer branches
of the hawthorn trees.

Evenings, I return to the peachglow
of street lamps, rain trickling
downhill, your thin wrists and
long hands peacefully folded
  on a lambsoft fleecy blanket.

THE AIRLINE TERMINAL

The hands on the clock move steadily toward seven.
Two cups of black coffee have lost their warmth.
Someone said that a moment of parting
should be one of composure, civility, acceptance.

The white points of your handkerchief . . .
dark blue suit . . . your brother's tie.
The rain outside may slacken soon.
Plane lights flicker there in the dark.

"It's seven now," you say with surprise.
The coffee check, there by the sugar bowl.
Hapless, my eyes spot your mangled teaspoon;
the human beast in my throat gives cry.

TAPS

At Union Station in Kansas City
on subways roaring across New York
by the waterbreak of a lake in Maine
the piñion pine on a hill near Taos
we met as lovers, then as friends,
spanning the years.
Now . . . again we come together
a few swift hours,
talk of war experiences,
time flowing,
essence and existence.

Of what has happened, another year
the scar on your face from a hit-and-run driver
a tiresome job which nearly defeated me
the failure of your marriages, third time try
your book finished, one thing accomplished
my sister's illness, her trip to Europe
your hair thinning, mine, gray . . .
passing moments, fragile clairvoyance

Time running out, journey's end
on a hill pitted by lonely stones
existence ending but a whisper somewhere
in the darkness ahead.
Standing sentinel to faraway train whistles,
listening for footsteps in darkened doorways,
I hear only
the sound of the trumpet
above the heave of the still night air.

A HOUSE ON A STREET

To cars that climb the concrete drive
the sign, FOR SALE, communicates
a market price and nothing more.
Across my brain the neon throb
of seven letters sails with pain.

Ghostly house, a different me
feels the slow inching of the past.
With brick and stone we tried to build
a rampart round our empty ease.
Breaks and cracks brought wintry cold.

A window glass without the sun
and vacant chairs that idly sit—
the castle of my mind calls out
for another life unmortised but spent.
I am deserting walls and roofs.

EXILES

The foghorn sounds
its hoarse loud cry
beneath the long,
silvery bridge
spanning the river.
Ship lights
sweep pale beams
across a black mirror,
cold waves undulating,
over and under,
under and over,
endlessly.
We shiver, turn,
stamp our feet
against the hard, wooden
floor of the deck.

Smokestacks puff
and jet a gray scud
against sky banked crosses
and sharp thin spires.
Untenanted faces
flash through window rounds
caroming the portholes
and passageways
like billiard balls
randomly cued.

Dreams and doorways
open and shut.
Long dresses swish
and glasses clink.
The ship rocks,
arms and legs couple,
turbulence of unfurling winds.
We stand on the threshold apart,
unstudied, unbound, undone.

GREEN AND SPRING

Nothing lasts, we said,
strolling hand in hand
along the banks of the Schuylkill.
We talk of direction,
friends, and the river's flow.
You tell me of the raincrashed
jungles of Vietnam.
I show you the cherry tree
where we once ate
Aunt Mary's poppyseed cake.
Smog, street crime, and drug dealers
blanket the city.
Barbara Streisand sings.

We gaze at the statue of William Penn.
Each day counts.
Our arms are young enough
to wallpaper a hospital,
our hearts wise enough
to know the risk of dreams.

The label on your bluejeans
reads Made in the U.S.A.
A bond of something
exists between us—
we're not sure what.
When Washington crossed the Delaware,
love of country stood beside him.
We stand again at the river's edge;
today flows and flowers into tomorrow.
Our lives bud
with green and spring.

CO-ED

She sprints around the campus
in a soft cotton jersey
and Calvin Klein jeans.
Her tangled curls
stream long and chestnut
in the cool morning breeze.
I look away, remembering
first steps and first words—
that she liked to go barefoot
up and down the stairs.

Adventure and romance
now fill her young dreams.
She blooms like a morning-glory,
open, startling, fresh, uncut.
She thinks about the Peace Corps
and talks of firewood,
vegetable gardens, tents, and huts.
I tend my green beans.

Someday I will leave her
my grandmother's star quilt,
an old oak dresser
my mother gave me,
the golden chain tree
I planted in the garden,
treasures enduring the wear of time.
She turns, smiles, goes her way;
I wave farewell to my co-ed child.

NORTHWEST OF YATES

Samuel Luke, "Papa"

I only knew him from a photograph,
mustache, dark eyes
behind gold rimmed spectacles,
dark hair swept away in deep waves
on both sides of a high part.
She called him "papa"
and sometimes told anecdotes,
what she could remember,
for he died
when she was eleven years old.
She looked very much like him.

He and his brother had a blacksmith shop,
and across the front, McCully Bros.
was printed in large black letters.
They wore leather aprons,
and she remembers his carpentry tools,
saws, chisels, brace and bits, level,
drawing knife and planers,
on the top shelf of a livingroom closet.
He played a tuba horn, wore a band uniform,
sang, and kept a tuning fork
in the oak dresser drawer.

In the wintertime he napped on the floor
behind the stove, and on rainy days
he half-soled their shoes.
Called away for jury duty,
he bought her a game of Rook
and a beautiful doll for his youngest.
She liked to go to the fields with him
and remembers the time she fell between
the iron wheels of a heavy farm wagon.
Her papa lifted the wheel
as it rolled over the length of her body.

Most of all, she remembers the night
he became very ill.
Riding the long tong rake,
he had raked hay all day.
Two doctors were called.
They said he should go
to St. Louis for surgery.
A spring wagon was backed to the door.
He called his four children to his bedside,
told them to mind their mama,
grandparents, and to meet him in heaven.
Then he was lifted onto a cot
and put in the spring wagon
for the trip to the depot.
The surgery was performed,
but he lived only a few hours.
He died at the age of 54 years and 23 days.

They went to the depot.
The train pulled in with the casket
on the platform of the baggage car.
A horse drawn hearse waited near by.
Mama wore black, and they were sad,
knowing how it would be without papa.
She was eleven, Leonard nine,
Josh, seven, and Kathryn, four.
She remembers that Mr. Jonas Robb
came off the train and told mama
their papa's last words,
"If I had the wings of an angel,
I would fly home to my loved ones."
She doesn't remember how long
her mama wore black,
but then mama never did go very much.

Amelia Christine, "Mama"

She was fifteen years younger
than her husband Sam,
Melie to her friends, mama to her children,
and Grandma Mac to her grandchildren.
Tall, big-boned, she walked outdoors
with a cane by the time I knew her.
She used the cane to smooth her bed covers
and sometimes gave it to us
for a stick horse to ride.

Her favorite chair
was a high backed cushioned rocker.
She could nap without breaking her neck.
The kitchen stove burned wood,
and she always rose early
to fix the breakfast, sometimes
wearing winter overshoes in the cold kitchen
until a noon sun warmed the room.
She made her own bread
from a barrel flour bin,
and the smell of fresh bread
wafted through the house.

Her days ticked by like the steady sound
of the clock on the mantlepiece. Tick tock.
The seasons came and went.
Days spent in cooking farm meals
three times a day, gathering eggs,
weaving carpet strips cut from worn overalls,
filling fresh straw in the ticks
under goose down feather beds,
milking cows in the summertime
when the men and boys worked
in the fields until dark.

Tick tock, the mantel clock.
Days spent washing clothes in soft water
caught in a wooden rain barrel,
nursing children with whooping cough,
burns and gashes,
churning golden round pounds of butter,
burying turnips, potatoes,
cabbage, and apples in the garden
under straw, dirt, and deep piles of snow,
teaching her children their A, B, C's,
how to count and read
in sleepy evenings around a warm stove.

Amelia held the family together,
two brothers helping
until the children were old and strong
enough for the hard work of a farm.
One brother, his head and left hand
badly burned, lived with them
the first two years after their papa died.
He brought his Bible and a few work clothes.
Meals were blessed, thanks given.

At Christmastime,
they had oranges and candy.
The four children survived,
bonded unbreakably.
Love flowed unspoken,
and a favorite hymn was "Gathering Home."

The Children

All four were born in Randolph County,
no hospitals then.
In their Sunday best,
they wore ruffled dresses
with gathers and lace,
hair ribboned long curls,
white shirts with pleated fronts,
wide embroidered collars,
tiny pearl buttons,
and high topped, laced black boots.

Old Clyde and Old Mag carried them
to a one room country school.
Old Clyde, a black mare
and the gentlest horse that ever lived.
Old Mag, fitful if she caught
her foot in the rein.
Then, climbing the nearest fence
to get out of her way was a scrambled must.
Old Fox was the first dog they had,
and he followed them to school.
Then Penny who had puppies
and Twister with his stump of a tail.

In summer they went barefoot,
climbed trees and fences,
waded in shallow creeks and streams,
peeked in birds' nests and down chimneys
to see chimney sweeps dart and cling.

At sheep shearing time,
the four watched but cried in a corner
to see a sheep thrown off its feet
and tied so it couldn't move.
Blood came if the shears nicked the sheep.
On nights that were cold,
the lean, naked sheep were brought
back to the fold and kept in the shed.

In winter, when the pond froze,
they ice skated until their legs ached.
In the deep woods
their papa cut down trees
and dragged chained logs
to the sawmill with horses and a lizard
while the ground was still frozen.
At the mill, a big, roaring
circular saw buzzed and cut off
four slabs to square the log,
then new planks.
With these their papa built a new barn.
They went to the mill only
if mama came along.

The local paper was delivered
to their mailbox once a week.
Mama would be sure to send one of them
to fetch the mail that day.
There was no telephone.
Going to school was a special event.
Old Clyde grew sick and weak.
When she could no longer lift her head
to drink or eat, their Uncle Albert
took a hammer and struck her dead
in the middle of the night.
The days, seasons, years ticked on.
Such were the stories told to me
by my first teacher and friend.
Those long nights passed,
and then the dawn.

OCTOBER BEACH

Walking the windswept beach
two fishermen come toward me,
        laughing and talking
in bridges of light, the silvery
sun spilling down the sky in
cloud castles and whitened towers,
        waist high boots slung
round their necks, brown bare feet
pressing downward the damp smooth sand,
        arms swinging the day's
bucket catch in measured gait,
heavensweep of friends living an
        October day's quiet splendor,
          moods that match,
            coming together.

            The fishermen pass.
High overhead the geese fly south,
distant black V-formations zagging
        the sky curve to warmer shores.
Down by the docks, ducks paddle roundly,
a symmetry of green heads circling and
reversing, cold fast water ballet.
            Seagulls cry
in the chambers of my distant dreams.
Bay waves lap against wooden pylons
reflected jaggedly in broken shadows.
        Two small boats rock
softly and gently, bumping one another.
Where will my heart find its harboring?

Late afternoon, a sword swath of sunlight
cuts across the water in a bright streak
of glitter, a shimmering long line of
diamond points
bouncing forward in chain linked fate.
Alone on the beach
with abandoned jellyfish, shattered shells,
tangles of black seaweed and bright green
ocean lettuce, I confront
the indifferent, cataclysmic roar and crash
of gray, ceaseless lashing waves.
Driftwood rides out to sea.
An iron spike sinks to burial
On invisible subterranean floors.

I gaze after the dark specks of the
two faraway fishermen,
foil to my solitary ways
and the seablown loss of my remembered
dark sunwashed friend.
Now only the chill October wind,
the whirring feet of tiny sea birds,
the roll and tumble of foaming breakers
cresting in tall blank white scrolls that
slowly unreel to thin watery
fans of receding crepe.

BEACHCOMBERS

Combing the seashore, wave carved and terraced
we roam for miles and sift the white silt,
bend to collect pale quartz crystals, pumiced
pink and red garnet in patterns occult.
Heaping sea pansies, lavender and luminant
anemones, sand dollars, moon snails and limpets
starfish, seawhips, conchs with horned crescent
sealace and rockweed for astral coronets.
Beached by spring tides with bottles and barrels
tossed from anchorage, planks, shells, and spars
drifting to shore despite many tangles . . .
finding existence on marginal floors.

Haiku

NEAR MY WINDOW

Long arms brush the pane,
Pink and white dogwood branches,
Spring returns again.

BELLE

Deep South and summer,
White magnolias' fragrant scent,
Dresses billowing.

HUMMINGBIRD

Swift, small colored blur
Wingbeats fast, a humming song
Borne toward flower's core.

SUMMER RAIN

Sheets of wetness crash
Down upon the parched dry land,
Grass blades purge and drink.

THROUGH THE FIELDS

Brown tasseled cornstalks,
Plowman's red bandanna waves
At trains passing by.

FAREWELL

Tissue thin, mild cheek,
Brown-mottled golden pear skin,
A mother's teardrop.

AUTUMN CALL

Snow geese overhead
Honking south to warmer shores,
White breasted kindred.

AMARYLLIS

Bright red majestic
Crown, towering scape with large
Gold threaded petals.

WINTER'S EVE

Snow covered high wire,
Tiny birds perched and balanced,
White treetops, still choir.